Rain Petitioning & Step Child Plays

Munyaradzi Mawere

Langaa Research & Publishing CIG
Mankon, Bamenda

Publisher:

Langaa RPCIG
Langaa Research & Publishing Common Initiative Group
P.O. Box 902 Mankon
Bamenda
North West Region
Cameroon
Langaagrp@gmail.com
www.langaa-rpcig.net

Distributed in and outside N. America by African Books Collective
orders@africanbookscollective.com
www.africanbookcollective.com

ISBN: 9956-790-70-2

DISCLAIMER
All views expressed in this publication are those of the author and do not necessarily reflect the views of Langaa RPCIG.

Acknowledgement

I wish to express my heartfelt thanks to Mr Wellington Charivanda for sparing his precious time to proof read the manuscript before it was send for publication

.

Table of Contents

Characters

Ambuya: A woman of about sixty years.

Bhaizani: A young man in his early twenties.

Chidhakwa: A fourty year old man who grew up in Harare, only to come back to his rural home after the 2005 'Operation Restore Order', dubbed 'Operation *Murambatsvina*'. He is a heavy drinker and is famous for senseless talks.

Gurukota: A man of about 55 years of age. He is the chief's councilor and/or adviser.

Mufundisi: A 42 year old man. He is a Minister in the church of Apostolic Faith Mission.

Mukadzi: A woman of about 40 years.

Murume: A man of about 38 years of age.

Musikana: A lady of about 21 years of age.

Reconcile: A man of about 33 years of age. He is pursuing his PhD studies overseas.

Muzvinasainzi: A 55 year old man. He is a scientist and lecturer at the University of Zimbabwe.

Nzarayauya: A 68 year old man, and is the village chief/traditional leader.

Pepukai: A young man in his mid twenties.

Povho: A large crowd from Nzarayauya village.

Sorojena: A man of about 80 years of age.

Sekuru: A man of about 75 years of age.

Dzidzisai: A 75 year old man. He is one of the chief's councilors responsible for leading ritual ceremonies such as the rain petitioning ceremony).

Vatendi: Christian believers in Nzarayauya's village.

Dare: Village body with judicial and executive authority to deliberate on issues affecting the community. Also, dare refers to a traditional village court.

Rain Petitioning

In Nzarayauya's village, famine and hunger strike as rain could not fall. The sky remains blue with scorching heat that leaves no creature desiring to move on with life. Chief Nzarayauya and his councillors believe this scourge is a curse from the ancestors. They think of holding a ceremony to mollify the ancestors and petition rain. The ceremony is held, but nothing happens except that hunger and famine strike even harder. This sets a fertile ground for conflict between traditionalists, Christians and scientists who lay blame on each other and take turns to intercede for the people. What comes out of this conflict only requires you to read the book for yourself.

1

Scene 1

Stage 1

(In this stage, we see villagers from Nzarayauya gathered at the village's court *(dare redunhu)*. The sun is scorching and there is no sign of rain coming any time soon. The villagers are discussing famine and hunger that have spread all over the village. They are planning to organize a rain petitioning ceremony for the ancestors).

Gurukota: (Making hollow-handed clapping). Good morning honorable chief Nzarayauya, the chief's councillors, ladies and gentlemen, and all others who have gathered around here. As you have been informed by the chief's messengers, this is a very important meeting for all the people in this village. Our honorable, chief Nzarayauya has important words he wants to share with all of us. My excellence, your people are waiting to hear from you. (Ululations and whistles as the chief stand up).

Nzarayauya: (Greeting dare). I am sure we all see that our land has been cursed. The rivers and streams used to flow throughout the year have all run dry. The sun blazes and scorches like nobody's business! Animals, plants and us people are all in the darkest moment of our lives. We can't continue folding our arms staring while our plants, animals and people surrender their lives to the Creator one by one. We have to take action and find out from our ancestors what have made them turn their backs to their children. But as we all know, ancestors are well respected beings. We can't just talk to them by word of mouth like I am doing to you right now. We need to brew beer first, beer to petition rain. This is the reason why I have summoned you here, so that we organize together when the beer can be brewed. (Ululations and whistles. Old women dance with excitement). Anyone against the idea of rain petitioning or who wants hunger and famine to continue haunting us?

Povho: (With one voice). *Hapana!* (No one!)

Nzarayauya: So if hunger is our common enemy, forward with rain petitioning! (Raising up his right clinched fist).

Povho: *Pamberi!* (Forward!) (Raising up their clinched fists).

Nzarayauya: *Pasi nenzara!* (Down with hunger!) (Dropping clinched fist).

Povho: *Pasi nayo!* (Down!) (Dropping clinched fists).

Nzarayauya: *Pamberi nemukweerera!* (Forward with rain petitioning ceremony!).

Povho: *Pamberi!* (Forward!).

Nzarayauya: We have all demonstrated that hunger is our number one enemy, and we all want to petition rain from our ancestors. Now each household in my village must bring a basketful of rapoko to my court-yard. All the rapoko should have been assembled by Friday next week so that they are soaked and beer is immediately brewed. Anyone against the idea of rain petitioning? Or with a question on this before I proceed? (A man who has just relocated to Nzarayauya's village raises his hand so that he can be granted permission to talk).

4

Murume: My salutations to our honorable chief, councillors and every one of you who have made every effort to attend this meeting. Honorable chief! (Looking at Nzarayauya). Thank you so much for your excellent words. Surely, everyone hates hunger. But I just want to know if even people like myself, who has just relocated to your village and have not had the first harvest in this village are also obliged to bring a basketful of rapoko? (Laughter from povho). That's all I wanted to know from my excellence. Thank you. (Hollow-handed clapping as he sits down).

Nzarayauya: A child who asks questions quests for wisdom. In our culture we say *'benzi bvunza rakanaka'* (A person who asks is not a fool but a lover of wisdom). But all I can say is that your question answers itself. If you relocated to this village and were allocated a portion to build your home and to cultivate, all it means is you also want rain to fall in your field if we petition it. When petitioning rain we don't ask ancestors to bring rainfall only to the fields of those who contributed rapoko for the ceremony. We want everyone to have enough food for his family. So everyone with a homestead and a field in this village should bring a basketful of rapoko for the *bira*/ceremony. If you personally don't have any rapoko, you ask from those who have. Isn't this our way of life? (Pointing at povho).

Povho: (One voice). That's it chief! (Noise as people talk to each other).

Nzarayauya: (Begging silence). Any other burning question before I proceed? (A young man, Bhaizani, raises up his hand).

Bhaizani: Thank you sir. I have heard your idea of rain petitioning, but it's in total contrast with what we studied at school. We learnt that it is not a person or ancestor who causes rain to fall. In fact it's well documented in the Geography books and my Geography teacher taught me that rain falls after a natural process whereby water evaporates into the atmosphere from plants and all water bodies it is found such as oceans, dams, rivers and streams. While in the atmosphere it condenses around small dust particles to form clouds. As this continues, the water particles in the atmosphere reach dew point such that they become heavy, and then rain falls. I can't see the causal relationship between ancestors and the falling of rain. Or do you mean that ancestors are the ones who command the water to evaporate, form clouds and fall? (Noise from the povho as some support and other opposes Bhaizani's position).

Gurukota: (Intervening). We are kindly asking for total silence. Silence everybody! The chief is still talking. (Silence observed).

Nzarayauya: Chief Nzarayauya shakes his head before responding to Bhaizani's concerns). This is what we mean when we say western education has spoilt our children. These schools brought forth by Whites are doing nothing except confusing the minds of our children. They teach what is contrary to our African reality, demonizing our culture. My child (pointing at Bhaizani), it's not your fault, but your teachers' fault. What they told you and read from your western based books only function there at school for you to pass your examinations. It doesn't work at all in our lives as black Africans. In fact it's a bunch of lies as far as our African reality is concerned. If it was true that the sun's heat and clouds are responsible for causing rain, then today we couldn't have been crying. Look how hot it is right now, but where is the rain? And the clouds! Aren't those clouds (pointing to the sky) we are all seeing, but where is the rain? If it is the dust you talked about, who didn't see the whirlwinds of this year? Isn't it whirlwind that demolished Mr Mushayi's homestead there? (Pointing to the direction of Mr Mushayi's homestead). So, why rain has not fallen? Isn't it that all this nullifies the lies you were told by your teachers? As long as our ancestors are angry with us, we will never get even a single drop. Even with the clouds, evaporation, and dust particles you have talked about. Is this not true people? (Pointing at povho).

Povho: (With one voice). That's it chief!

Nzarayauya: *Pamberi nekunzwisisa!* (Forward with understanding!) (Raising up his clinched fist).

Povho: *Pamberi!* (Forward!) (Raising up their clinched fists).

Nzarayauya: *Vasingazivi?* (Those who are ignorant?)

Povho: (With one voice). *Ngavadzidziswe!* (Must be taught!)

Nzarayauya: Anyone who didn't understand what I have explained to this child? (Pointing at Bhaizani).

Povho: (One voice). No one!

Nzarayauya: If we all agree to what I have said, that's good. I will proceed to ask all the old women - those who no longer procreate - and the virgin girls to brew the beer for the rain petitioning for us. This does not mean that all others will be seated while preparations are being made. All other women will be responsible for ferrying water to brew the beer. But the night before the day set for this work to commence, none of you is allowed to sleep with her husband. These are the inviolables of the rain petitioning beer brewing. Otherwise you will frustrate and anger our ancestors. (Some brief noise is heard). All the young men shall be responsible for gathering firewood to brew the beer. We want excellent wood. You will have to climb on top of that hill, Chiwadzi (pointing at the hill) where there is good wood. As I previously pointed out, next Friday preparations for this ceremony should commence. Any question on this? (One old woman raises up her hand).

Ambuya: My salutations to our honorable chief, his councillors and all others at this meeting. Mine is just a small observation. I have heard my honorable mentioning the duties of all other age groups, but seem to have forgotten the old men. Will these be folding their hands and watch as we will be working? That's all I wanted to know. (Sitting down).

Nzarayauya: You have asked a very good question grandma. As we all know, everyone in this village has a mouth and stomach to feed. So everyone who is still able bodied will participate in one way or another. The work and the ceremony belong to us all. Some of the old men will prepare the shade of that big baobab tree in that hill. (Pointing at the hill). Like all other years, this is the place where the rain petitioning ceremony will be held. The other old men will monitor the preparations and lead the ceremony itself. So no one will be seated. Isn't it people?

Povho: *Ndizvozvo vashe!* (That's it chief!)

Nzarayauya: *Pamberi nemukweerera!* (Forward with rain petitioning ceremony!)

Povho: *Pamberi!* (Forward!)

Nzarayauya: *Pasi nenzara!* (Down with hunger!)

Povho: *Pasi nayo!* (Down with it!)

Nzarayauya: *Pamberi nemaguta!* (Forward with bump harvest!)

Povho: *Pamberi!* (Forward!)

Nzarayauya: I am confident that all of us here have agreed on what we should do to fight our number one enemy, hunger, in this village. Is there anyone still having a burning question before we call off our meeting?

Povho: (One voice). No one! We have all understood. (People dispersing).

Stage II

(It is around 9 o'clock in the morning. Old women enter the stage balancing pots of beer on their heads. Mr Dzidzisai is the master of ceremony, instructing women where to put their pots. Other people are singing outside the stage).

Dzidzisai: (Begging silence). My greetings to our honorable chief, his dedicated councillors, grandpas, grandmas, fathers, mothers and every one of you who is present at this ceremony. Before presenting the ceremony's agenda, I will ask our honorable chief to give opening words, and to thank you all for cooperating in this important event. To you chief! (pointing to chief Nzarayauya).

Nzarayauya: *Pamberi nemukweerera!* (Forward with rain petitioning ceremony!)

Povho: (One voice). *Pamberi!* (Forward!).

Nzarayauya: *Pamberi nemaguta!* (Forward with bumper harvest!)

Povho: (One voice). *Pamberi!* (Forward!)

Nzarayauya: *Pamberi nekunzwisisa!* (Forward with understanding!)

Povho: *Pamberi!* (Forward!)

Nzarayauya: It is a great pleasure and excitement to have a big day such as this, a day that we all expect to completely change our situation. To start with, I would like to thank our

11

ancestors and God for having guided and giving us a spirit of team work during preparations for this ceremony. I also want to thank you all for working hard to have this ceremony materialize. My special thanks to our grandmothers, young women and men, and all who cooperated during the preparation phase of this ceremony. Keep up this good spirit. This is all I wanted to say. We will hear the rest from our Master of ceremony, Mr Dzidzisai. Thank you! (Round of applause).

Dzidzisai: Thank you. Thank you. I will remind you that this is a ceremony to petition rain from our ancestors. Our ancestors, you Pfupajena over there, Mazarura, Manenga, Mupazvose and all others in the Mabweadziva shrine we cannot mention by names, this is the beer your children have prepared for you. Quench your thirst. (He draws beer using a ladle and sips a little bit before he pours the other beer on the ground and passes the ladle to chief and the chief's councillors in order of their traditional ranks). But please remember us your children. We want rain. Our animals, trees and we people are facing death. You can't let us down. We are your children. (Facing the crowd). We can sing a song while we are waiting for mothers to bring sadza/stiff porridge. I just feel sorry for the greedy and 'meat lovers' because sadza for a ceremony such as this cannot be eaten with meat. (Laughter, then a rain petitioning song called *dhonyori*).

Vocalist: *Vanotambira pakarimwa.*

Backing Vocals: *Dhonyoriwe dhonyori.*

V: *Vanotambira pakarimwawe.*

BV: *Dhonyoriwe dhonyori, dhonyo dhonyori.*

V: *Tinotambira pakarimwa chete.*

BV: *Dhonyoriwe dhonyori, tinotambira pakarimwa.*

V: *Tinotambira pakarimwawe.*

BV: *Dhonyoriwe dhonyori, tinotambira pakarimwa.*

(People stop singing as women enter the stage holding plates of sadza prepared from rapoko meali-meal).

Dzidzisai: Our honorable chief, councillors and all of us around here, our catering team have brought us some food to enjoy ourselves before we start drinking and dancing. Our grandmothers and daughters brew us first rate beer. After finishing all these (pointing to dozens of pots of beer) here, we will go and drink the other beer left at our honorable chief's court yard. As per our tradition, beer for the small rats *(doro retukonzo),* has already been set aside. We will 'see' it tomorrow morning. Just a word of advice: here in a ceremony such as this anything goes. No one should be driven mad. If a fight or quarrel breaks out, our ancestors will get annoyed, and no rain will fall down. We will have wasted our efforts and our petite resources. In short, this is our program line-up. Anyone who didn't understand how our ceremony goes? (A man with scruffy hair, Chidhakwa raises his hand).

Chidhakwa: Thank you my greatness. To start with, I want to thank the organizers of this ceremony. Some of us here have filled our tummies for the first time since last year when famine struck. (Laughter from povho). All other things are in

13

the right direction except one thing. I didn't like the idea of *doro retukonzo*, giving beer to rats! With all the famine here, can you surely afford to give beer to rats leaving aside people like us? (Laughter from povho).

Dzidzisai: (Smiling). You have asked a good question my son. Some of you still have milk on the nose. Others are attending a ceremony such as this for the first time. As future leaders, you surely need to understand all bits and pieces of the event. I am sure most of you- the new generation- do not understand what we mean by *doro retukonzo* (beer for the small rats). *Doro retukonzo* is beer that is presented before the ancestors as a way of showing our loyalty during the rain petitioning ceremony. This is done by grandmothers and village elders. Right now as I speak, we have already presented the beer before our ancestors. They will drink only a little of this beer, and the rest we will drink it ourselves tomorrow morning. Anyone who likes the beer can drink it freely except the little children we have also prohibited from attending this ceremony. These, because of age are not allowed to drink beer. Is there still anyone with a question before we start drinking?

Povho: (One voice). No one!

Dzidzisai: If no question, that's fine. It's a sign that our ceremony is progressing well, and that our ancestors will hear us. We hope we will soon receive rain. (Ululations and whistles, others begin singing a rain petitioning song).

Vocalist: *Vadzimu vedu musazokanganwa kuti vana venyu tinodawo mvura.* (Our ancestors do not forget that we your children need rain water).

14

Backing Vocalists: *E-he, vadzimu vedu musazokanganwa.* (Sure, our ancestors don't forget!)

V: *Vadzimu vedu musazokanganwa kuti vana venyu tinoda maguta.* (Our ancestors do not forget that we your children need a bumb harvest).

BV: *E-he, vadzimu vedu musazokanganwa.* (Sure, our ancestors don't forget!)

V: *Vadzimu vedu musazokanganwa kuti tinoda donhodzo.* (Our ancestors do not forget that we need to be cooled)

BV: *E-he, vadzimu vedu musazokanganwa.* (Sure, our ancestors do not forget). (Ululations and whistles as people are dancing).

Stage III

(A month has elapsed after the rain petitioning ceremony was held. No rain falls. People from Nzarayauya's village are again at a *dare* (village court/meeting place). At the *dare* arise serious conflicts as people disagree on many issues about the famine and hunger in the village).

Nzarayauya: (Greetings everyone). I am sure you all know that last month we had a rain petitioning ceremony in this village. As we all know nothing has changed yet especially for the better. Instead, things are getting worse day by day. I don't know if someone bewitched us or is there anyone with an idea as to why the ancestors have turned their backs on us? In Shona we say, *"mazano marairanwa"* (*lit,* Good ideas are shared). So I have called you upon that we can share ideas on what else can be done to change our situation. (Whispers from the people. One old woman, Ambuya raises up her hand).

Ambuya: Well, I think all we need to do now is to send you (our chief) and other village elders to go and seek advice from 'Manyusa' (rain spirits). Those ones know better than anyone else especially on why rain did not come when the rain petitioning ceremony was held. I am sure the Manyusa will give us the right direction. This is my small contribution. Thank you. (Some ululations and whistles of approval as Ambuya sits down). (One young man raises his hand to be given a platform).

Mukomana: I stand to differ from what Ambuya has said. The reason being that before the rain petitioning ceremony was held, these Manyusa were asked to advise the village on whether it was proper to go ahead with the ceremony. I am

17

told they all said rain petitioning was the only way our ancestors would hear us on the rain issue. They added that the ceremony was going to be held peacefully and rain will fall on the evening of the 'D-Day'. So what other advice do we still need from these Manyusa? I think it will be a waste of time for us to go back to the same Manyusa who have already failed to predict our future, and change our situation. Personally, I do not think the drought we are facing is a curse from our ancestors. Rain falls (or do not fall) naturally. The reason for the drought is severe deforestation that is going on in the entire village. Deforestation disturbs the natural phenomena that cause rain to fall. There is no other reason at all. (Some noises and grumbles from the majority, while a few others whistle in approval). (One old man raises up his hand).

Sekuru: (Shaking his head). As far as I know, *'Njuzu'* (Water spirits/Mermaids) are the ones with the final say on rain issues, not the Manyusa or the natural phenomena. They have powers to cause rain or to stop it from falling, especially when they are unhappy with what we people are doing. When angry, they can cause all water bodies except in those areas where they reside to dry up until we have paid reparation. What Ambuya has suggested is none event, as long as we haven't paid reparations to the *Njuzu*. Worse still what my 'son' here has said. The natural phenomena he talked about are controlled by some big forces like *Njuzu* that control everything to do with rain water. The Manyusa can only help if there is no problem between us and the *Njuzu*. Remember the Manyusa themselves are powerless before *Njuzu*. Some of them even get their powers from the *Njuzu*. As such, I think the best we should do is to approach the *N'angas* with Mermaid spirit. These can talk directly to the *Njuzu* and hear if we wronged the latter, and what actually needs to be done to control our situation. If we know what needs to be done from such reliable mediums, I am sure our problem will soon be history. Once done, the *Njuzu* will unlock their 'rain locks' and let the rain fall down like nobody's business. And this has to be done as a matter of urgency. Otherwise, we will have more questions to answer before the *Njuzu* and our ancestors. Look! Right now, plants and animals are suffering simply because of us humans. (Some people ululate and whistle in approval but others shake their heads in disapproval). (Mufundisi from Apostolic Faith Mission Church raises up his hand).

Mufundisi: (Thoughtfully). I beg to differ with what all the previous speakers have said. I do not see any of what they have said helping us in any way besides extending our problem. I remain very concerned that most of us still believe in some creatures other than God. God is the source of our life and everything on earth including the *Njuzu* and our subject of talk here, rain water. As my brother here (pointing to the young man who spoke before him) rightfully said, the Manyusas are the ones who advised how the rain petitioning ceremony should be held. And, this did not give any positive result. This alone shows that Manyusa have no power over nature. As for the *Njuzu*, they are just creatures like us human beings. They were also created by God who has power over everything on earth and heaven. They have no power over rain as Sekuru have said. What my brother here have said is also incredible. Since we were born in this village, trees have always been cut for fuel wood, constructing poles and farm extension. But ever since, rain has always been abundant. Besides, in all the mountains around here trees are abundant. Why then rain is not falling in those mountains if it is the trees that cause rain to fall? (Noise as some people approves

19

of and others disapprove of Mufundisi's words. Mufundisi goes on). As I have already highlighted, I am sure God alone has the power to command rain to fall or not to fall. So what is better for us is to call Christian churches to come unto this village and pray for us. If we do this, I am sure rain will fall without any delay. Thank you. (Some people murmur in approval but others disapprovingly shout in high pitched voices. Chief Nzarayapera intervenes and wraps up the debate).

Nzarayauya: *'Hadzirimi asi kuti dzinonzwa'*. (They do not till, but hear). I have heard all your views. From all the contributions given, there is no doubt that the issue at stake is a hard nut to crack. We shouldn't rush. Otherwise, we will aggravate the situation that is already bad. In short, I think we cannot conclude this issue today at this dare. I need more time to sit down with my councillors and village elders to decide the way forward, but based on the different opinions that have been given here. After this, we will send messengers around the village calling you all for another meeting. I therefore declare this meeting over- until our next meeting! (People disperse in groups, supporting different views given during the meeting).

Scene 2

Stage I

(It is during the day in Nzarayauya's village. Mufundisi (Minister) of *Apostolic Faith Mission* is preaching at a church gathering assembled to pray for the rain. They all pray in loud voices).

Mufundisi: Halleluiah!

Christians: Amen!

Mufundisi: Forward!

Christians: Ever!

Mufundisi: Up! Up!

Christians: Jesus!

Mufundisi: Down with....!

Christians: Satan!

Mufundisi: Forward!

Christians: Ever!

Mufundisi: I want to greet and welcome you all in the name of Jesus. Initially, I would like to thank God for permitting us to meet here. Our God is a God of love, peace and unity. He loves us his children. He is responsible for all good things and Satan is responsible for all bad things- deaths and sufferings-on earth. Halleluiah!

Christians: Amen!

Mufundisi: I am sure we all know that we are facing the problem of drought in this area. Plants, animals and we humans are all in 'tried moments' due to drought. All these are works of the devil whose aim is to frustrate us so that we turn away from God. Satan thinks that if we suffer, then we would seize to believe in a God who let us suffer. It is the same Satan who tempted the biblical Job and cursed him with all sorts of evil. He wanted to frustrate Job so that he would think his God is uncaring. He is the same Satan who came through Job's wife and persuaded him to curse the Lord God so that he is healed of his wounds. He is the same Satan holding water from falling down in an attempt to frustrate and turn our hearts away from our loving God. So, today we want to pray to our God that He forsake us not; that He don't let us tempted by Satan, and that rain falls in this area before dawn tomorrow. Halleluiah!

Christians: Amen! (All people begin praying in loud voices, with Mufundisi's voice at the top of all others).

Mufundisi: Oh Lord, our Most High God. You are a wonderful God. You are a loving and caring Father. We all come unto you this afternoon crying for forgiveness, crying for deliverance from evil, and crying for victory over Satan. Look Oh Lord, the menace of the devil! It is threatening the lives you gave us for free! Hunger and thirsty are all troubling us oh Lord. Don't forsake us. We are your children. Today we pray unto you Lord. That you send us heavy rains before the end of the day! Let things return to normalcy. We all want a bumb harvest, peace and prosperity. Don't let us down, oh Lord. We are your children. Amen! (Mufundisi starts singing a song called *'matikanganwa'* (you have forsaken us).

Mufundisi: *Seiko matikanganwa Jehovah?* (Why have you forsaken us Lord?)

Brethren: *Matikanganwa Jehovah, matikanganwa.* (You have forsaken us Lord, you have forsaken us).

M: *Matikanganwa seiko, matikanganwa Jehovah?* (Why have you forsaken us, why have you forsaken us Lord?).

B: *Matikanganwa Jehovah, matikanganwa.* (You have forsaken us Lord, you have forsaken us).

M: *Isu takabata muzita renyu!* (When we delivered/worshipped in your name!)

B: *Matikanganwa Jehovah, matikanganwa.* (You have forsaken us Lord, you have forsaken us).

M: *Nezuva iro vanhu vachati kuna Jehovah taiporofita muzita renyu baba, tichidzinga mweya yetsvina muzita renyu wani, seiko matikanganwa?* (On that day people would say to God, 'But we prophesied in your name Lord, exorcising demons in your name?'

B: *Matikanganwa Jehovah, matikanganwa.* (You have forsaken us Lord, you have forsaken us).

M: *Chiregai kutikanganwa Jehovah musatikanganwa.* (Now do not forsake us Lord, do not forsake us).

B: *Musatikanganwa Jehovah, musatikanganwa.* (Do not forsake us Lord, do not forsake us). (People stop singing, and Mufundisi continues preaching the word of God).

Mufundisi: Our God is a God of miracles. He has power to command mountains to move from one place to another. He also has the power to command oceans to move from one place to another. The cause of us being here is to ask our God to command rain to fall by the end of the day. Through faith we will witness miracles here, rain will fall before end of day. Remember, through faith the blind man at Bethsaida was commanded by Jesus to open his eyes, and he saw. Through faith, Peter and John commanded the lame to walk, and he walked. Also, through faith we request that God command rain to fall before the end of the day. Halleluiah!

Christians: Amen! (Again, Mufundisi leads people in prayer. They pray in loud voices but with Mufundisi's voice above all others).

Mufundisi: Our Lord God in heaven, we thank you for creating us as humans with reason and intelligence that surpasses those of all other animals on earth. As the creator of earth and heaven, we know you have power over everything. You are like a master key that unlocks all locks. Even Satan and his demons are afraid of you Lord. We therefore pray unto you to roar with your frightening voice. That Satan will run away from the mouth of heaven and let rain fall. We pray with all our hearts Lord that rain falls before end of today. We know you have powers to perform miracles. You are the all-powerful God who gave Joshua the power to command the sun to stop, and it stopped. Through our faith and your power, we believe we will receive rain before the end of the day. We leave all this unto you and your only son Jesus Christ and the Holly spirit. Amen! (Mufundisi sings a song to bid farewell - *'rwiyo rwekuyenekana'*).

Mufundisi: *Vanotenda sarai zvakanaka.* (Brethren, stay well!).

Brethren: *Tava kuenda.* (As we leave).

M: *Vanosara sarai zvakanaka.* (Those who are staying behind, stay well).

B: *Tava kuenda.* (As we leave).

M: *Vanoenda, fambai zvakanaka.* (Those who are leaving, go well).

B: *Mava kuenda.* (As you leave).

M: *Fambai zvakanaka.* (Go well).

B: *Mava kuenda.* (As you leave). (People bid farewell, each of them taking his way home).

Stage II

(Again, it is in Nzarayauya's village. It is now about three weeks after Mufundisi and his people gathered to pray for rain. Until this time, nothing has happened. The people decide to call a Scientist, Muzvinasainzi, from the University of Zimbabwe to explain the cause of the drought).

Nzarayauya: My greetings to all my councillors, village elders and all of you present at this meeting. As I promised you in our previous meeting, my councillors, elders and I sat down to chat the way forward with the issue of drought. One of our village elders, Mr Tandangu has his son, a renowned scientist at the biggest university in this country, University of Zimbabwe. He obtained his chains of degrees in Geography and Environmental Sciences at one of the most famous and prestigious universities in the world, University of Cambridge. Besides, he is an author of several books on environmental issues. When we heard about his rich curriculum by his father, we, as a *dare* decided to call him upon to explain his understanding of the causes of droughts such as this. We will have to listen attentively as we hear big words coming from the respectable Muzvinasainzi. (Some people ululate, others whistle excitedly as Muzvinasainzi stands up).

Muzvinasainzi: (Composed). Thank you! Well, as you have heard from our honorable chief, Mr Nzarayauya saying, I am a Professor, an expert in Geographical and environmental sciences. (Round of applause from povho). I am sure all of us here are concerned with the drought we are facing. Some of us lay blame on others or even to ourselves thinking that we are the ones causing erratic rainfalls all these years. Of course, some but not all of us play a role in causing erratic rainfall. Do we want to know what causes erratic rainfalls and an increase of heat in the atmosphere or what we call global warming?

Povho: (One voice). Yes, that is what has brought us here!

Muzvinasainzi: Ok. I will start by explaining the causes of global warming we are all experiencing the world over. This is caused by the constant increase of heat in the atmosphere resulting in the destruction of the ozone layer- a layer that protects us from the sun rays. From the research we scientists carried out, we discovered that the ozone layer is being destroyed, though slowly. The major causes for this destruction are anthropogenic activities including gas emissions from motor vehicles and industries which release gases into the atmosphere. In short, this is what causes global warming-the unbearable and intensified heat we are all experiencing. Anyone who has a question on global warming before I explain the causes of erratic rainfalls and droughts we are experiencing these days? (People nod their heads in approval, others whistle). (One young lady, Musikana, raises up her hand to ask a question).

Musikana: Thank you so much Professor for the explanation you have given. I am sure most of us here were ignorant of the causes of global warming: a problem that is increasingly threatening life on earth in many ways. You have done quite well in your explanation. All what I want to know is whether it is the industries and vehicles alone that cause global warming.

Muzvinasainzi: (Scratching his head, smiling). You have asked a very good question my sister. Well, not only the industries and vehicles are responsible for global warming. We have a host of other causers including veld fires and even the fire we make every day for cooking. In fact, anything that produces gas into the atmosphere is capable of causing global warming and by extension damaging the ozone layer which just like the layer that protects our eyes is very sensitive. This is one reason why people are nowadays encouraged to adopt pollution free sources of energy such as solar and electricity for cooking and heating. Any other question before I proceed?

Povho: (One voice). No question. Please go ahead!

Muzvinasainzi: Now I am coming on to the central issue that has brought all of us here: the causes of erratic rainfalls and droughts. There is no one answer here as there are a plethora of factors including global warming itself. The issue of global warming, for example, is causing the melting of ice at the poles and excessive evapotranspiration. This in turn results in floods and disruption of the rainfall pattern as well as climate change. With these changes, it is possible to receive rainfall in those months we used not to receive even a single drop such as August and vice versa, hence the drought such as the one we are experiencing. In other words, the rainfall becomes unreliable and thus erratic. Anyone unhappy with my response on the causes I have explained so far? (No one raises his hand, but some few individuals show a sign of discontentment. They grumble and whisper to one another).

Povho: (One voice). No one!

Muzvinasainzi: Fine, if you have all understood my first point. The other cause of erratic rainfall is deforestation. All these green trees (pointing to some trees nearby) we all see assist in the hydrological cycle by emitting some vapour- transpiration- into the atmosphere. This vapour combines with the one from water bodies such as oceans to form clouds which ultimately bring us rainfall. So because of deforestation that takes place yearly, the amounts of water vapour in the atmosphere continue to decrease resulting in erratic rainfalls and droughts. In this respect, we people are the causers of unreliable rainfalls and droughts. This is one reason why we are discouraged from practising deforestation. (Some noise as people grumble. A young man, Pepukai then raises up his hand).

Pepukai: Thank you. I agree with the first cause you explained, but not with the second one (Noise that take some time to settle before Pepukai proceeds). The reason why I disagree with your explanation is that even in the mountains in this area and beyond, where there are big and tall trees no rain falls. Why the rain can't at least fall in those places with trees and leave those without? Besides, in the past our forefathers used to cut down trees around here as they practised shifting cultivation, but rain always fell without any problem! Worse still, the big rivers around here that contribute towards the formation of clouds as you have explained have not received even a single drop! So I don't agree with your explanation, especially on the second cause. (Some more noise as other people support with Pepukai's view. Others disagree. Chief Nzarayauya sees that there might be a serious conflict. He declares the meeting adjourned).

Nzarayauya: (Begging silence). Like what happened at the previous meeting, I can still see that we do not have a universal or common solution to our problem at hand. We still need some more time to digest the issue to come up with a lasting solution. That said, I will declare the meeting closed. I will have to sit down once again with my councillors and elders to map the way forward. We will always keep you informed. (Noise as people disperse).

Stage III

(It is at Chief Nzarayauya's courtyard. There is a councillors' meeting with the chief. Reconcile, chief Nzarayauya's son who is studying towards PhD in Social Anthropology overseas is on holiday. He is also part of the meeting).

Nzarayauya: (Welcoming and greeting everybody). I have summoned you here to discuss further the issue that has boggled the minds of us all in this village- the issue of rain. We did the rain petitioning ceremony, but nothing happened! The Christians interceded for the village, but no rain came! Only two weeks ago, we asked a Professor from the University of Zimbabwe to tell us what he thinks about our situation but the majority disagreed with his thinking. With all these concerted efforts, our situation is even worsening day by day. Now, my councillors and elders gathered here are our gateways of knowledge. You have vast experiences of life. What do you think we should do to arrest this situation that is threatening to devour our lives? Shall we just watch while hunger and famine spread their tentacles in the entire village? We should come up with a wise idea that will solve this problem once and for all. We all need rain. We all want to move on with life. What shall we do? (One old man, Sorojena raises up his hand).

Sorojena: (Greeting *dare* according to tradition). It is true that the rainfall pattern we are experiencing these years is very confusing. Even though, hunger and famine have caught us unaware. If I can still remember well, since I was born in 1920 drought as severe as this one only occurred twice, I think between 1947and 1949 and in 1992. As far as I

33

remember, people kept on petitioning rain from our ancestors. On the other hand, Christians also prayed unceasingly for the rain. Even the so-called 'moderns', who believe in science alone played their part. We used to hear from the radio that these scientists were planting clouds here and there. And the years that followed the drought came bumb harvests that no old man had witnessed before. What only confused me after the drought is that the three parties (traditionalists, Christians and scientists) started a war of words. Each of these groups claimed to have been the one who caused rain to fall. Traditionalists were quoted to have been saying "We are the ones who talked to our ancestors and God to bring rainfall". On a different note, Christians could be heard saying: "We talked to our angels and God to bring rainfall on earth after recognizing that plants, animals and humans would soon surrender their lives". In the radios and newspapers, the issue that kept hitting the headlines was: "Scientists have successfully caused rain to fall after their cloud seeding activities". The truth is no one knew what really caused the rain to fall after the severe droughts. Most of us just stood by the old people's adage that: "*Mushure menzara munouya maguta*/After famine always come bumb harvests". So I am not very sure of what actually should we do to solve our problem, but perhaps we can think with the experiences I have given you. (Sorojena sits down. Reconcile raises up his hand).

Reconcile: (Greeting *dare*). Of course my grandfather here (pointing at Sorojena) did not tell us what exactly should we do, but in other words he told us. He has given us good framework and direction which should be followed to address problems such as the one at hand. This is exactly what we learn at university. What I have liked most from grandpa's speech is that he clearly showed us that during the previous droughts, everyone –whether a Christian, a scientist or a traditionalist - participated in the fight against drought depending on what they believed in. None of them waited that so and so will provide solutions for them. As grandpa told us, traditionalists fought their own way. Christians on the other hand played their part, and likewise scientists. (People nod their heads in approval). The other important thing our grandpa has underlined is that the truth about the previous droughts is that no one exactly knew what ultimately caused rain to fall. But what remains clear is that everyone wanted rain to fall. As such, what all the three parties - Christians, traditionalists and scientists- did helped in one way or another to end the droughts. Thank you! (Whispers while other councillors and elders nod their heads in approval. One of the chief's councillors raises up his hand).

Councillor: (Begging silence). I think this young man (pointing at Reconcile) has said something very important words. If we follow his advice, we will certainly be able to end this perilous drought. And, if we present such wise words to the majority of the people in this village, I am sure they will all agree. His words, like his name, reconcile all the three contenting parties – Christians, traditionalists and scientists. None of them is offended. I think what we need to do is to give this young man enough time to explain his position to the people at dare. Otherwise, we will continue failing to convince our people. The end result is that we will lose their hearts and respect as their leaders. (Ululations and whistles of approval at the *dare*. The dare asks Reconcile to go ahead with his explanation).

Dare: (One voice). Let him go ahead!

Reconcile: Thank you. I can proceed to say that our major problem in this area is that of looking down upon others, especially between those of us with divergent views. You know when western imperialists infiltrated into our country and generally in Africa, they despised our traditional values. In place of these values, science was offered as the universal and most legitimate value system. Most of our black Africans started to look down upon their own traditions. This has been the same with Christianity when it was brought to us by the Missionaries. The latter assumed that Africans had no idea of God and, therefore, taught us to hate everything linked to our traditional religion. With this, I do not mean that tradition is the best of all. Neither am I saying Christianity or science is the best. For the Westerners or anyone who wholeheartedly believe in Christianity, it perfectly works. So is science and tradition. For all those who believe in either of them with all their hearts, it works. All what it means is that the three are equally important to their respective believers. Besides, each one of them has its own challenges. So I think what is bad between believers in the three groups is to look down upon each other. We need to understand that even in this country people have different jobs or areas of specializations. Some are teachers; others are policemen, nurses and so on. They help each other for common good- to have a better world. They don't walk around mocking each other as believers in the three groups do. This is the same example believers in Christianity, tradition and science should follow. You have to exercise tolerance because as my grandpa here rightly pointed out when he talked about the previous droughts, no one knew who exactly caused rain between the three groups. That said,

I think this is what people in this village should do to end the drought. Traditionalists should continue asking for rain their own way. Christians and scientists should also do likewise. Thank you. (A round of applause from *dare* as Reconcile re-takes his seat. Sorojena stands up to give a vote of thanks).

Sorojena: (Thanking). I think our son here (pointing at Reconcile) has played it all. He has given us an excellent idea which I think none of our people will object in our next meeting with them. That's why our elders say: *"Azvara honho azvara mhare"*. He is a deep thinker- a think tank of our time! Amongst the councillors and elders gathered here, is there anyone with a better idea than this one?

Dare: (One voice). No one!

Sorojena: Sure, I agree. Our honourable chief, elders and councilors, I think our issue is well grounded. *"Nyaya yedu yaibva iyi"*. You can give your final word. (Chief Nzarayauya stands up, smiling).

Nzarayauya: If no one disagrees this is what we are going to tell our people the next time we meet them. I am confident that the Christians, traditionalists and those who believe in science will all embrace the idea. The merit of this position is that it doesn't despise any person's view. Instead, it places all views- from scientists, Christians and traditionalists- at the same plane. So, all of our people are likely to endorse the idea. With this, I declare the meeting over. Until the day we meet our people. (Ululations and whistles as *dare* disperse).

-END-

Step-child

In chief Ziki's chiefdom arises an issue that boggles the minds of many people. While the story provokes amusement to some, to others it provokes tears. The story is about one step-son, Mubvandiripo, who grow up with a step-father in the Chitsa area. The step-son only knows of the ordeal after the death of his 'father' when he is told that he will not inherit anything from the deceased because he is not a legitimate son. Moved by the incident, Mubvandiripo starts a long painful journey looking for his real father. He arrives at his father's home the second day after his [father] burial, only to find his kinships in a meeting to divide the deceased's estate. What do you think later happens to the [real] father's estate? Did Mubvandiripo get any share?.... It only needs the reader to read for himself!

Characters

Mubvandiripo: The main character of the story. He is the legitimate/biological son of Chenjerai and Rambisai.

Chenjerai: The husband of Rambisai, and the real father of Mubvandiripo.

Takurai: The man who marries Maidei after divorced by Chenjerai.

Maidei: The woman divorced by Chenjerai, and later remarries Takurai.

Babamukuru: Takurai's elder brother.

Babamunini: Chenjerai's only brother. He is younger than Chenjerai.

Tete: Chenjerai's sister.

Mwana: A girl of about 8 years, and is the daughter of Chenjerai and Rambisai.

Rambisai: Chenjerai's wife.

Govai: Takurai's eldest nephew.

Enzanisai: Chenjerai's eldest nephew.

Mbuya: Takurai's mother.

Maonei: Chenjerai's mother.

Marujata: Chenjerai's aunt.

Takudzwa: A young boy of about 11, and is the eldest son of Chenjerai and Rambisai.

Rudo: A girl of about 15, and she is Chenjerai and Rambisai's first born daughter.

Scene 1

Stage I

(It is dusk at Chenjerai's homestead in chief Ziki's chiefdom. Maidei, who is pregnant, is accompanied by her aunt to marry Chenjerai according to the Shona customary marriage of *kuganha*. Like a dog, Maidei is chased by Rambisai, Chenjerai's wife.)

Mwana: (Panting). Mum! Mum! There are two people seated by the pathway from the cattle pen. One of them is in white quilt.

Rambisai: Ah! I know you are always frightened with small things. You are hen hearted. People! Looking for what by the cattle pen? Who are they?

Mwana: I am not lying mum! I do not know who are they and what they want. I greeted them, but did not respond. I am afraid, they are two. (Raising up two fingers of her right hand).

Rambisai: (Calling loudly). Ba Rudo! Hey baba Rudo!

Chenjerai: (Getting out of his bedroom). Don't you know that I am tired? But you know that I have been toiling the whole day! Is all well that you disturb my rest?

Rambisai: It's not well my dear! I am told there are people seated by our cattle pen. Go and check who they are and what do they want. Don't you think these are the notorious thieves that are causing havoc in this village? Only yesterday

43

they stole two chickens and a he-goat from Mufaro's homestead. Please be quick! We may get at the cattle pen only to see cow dung. Otherwise the thieves are only waiting for it to be darker. Don't leave your axe and knobkerrie behind. They can attack us.

Chenjerai: (Loud voice). People seated! Looking for what by the cattle pen? Did they identify themselves?

Rambisai: Hey baba Rudo! You are delaying. You keep on asking what I have already told you! I do not know who they are and what they want. I asked you to take your axe and knobkerrie, lest they are thieves. I am told those who stole at Mufaro last night ran away after dishing Mufaro a blow that left him temporarily blind! Be quick baba Rudo, our cattle will go. (Rambisai follows behind her husband holding a knobkerrie as well).

Chenjerai: (Gross voice, but from a distant). Are you lost? Who are you and what do you want at my cattle pen?

Tete: I am Chenjerai. We are not lost at all. We are looking for a path that takes us to your home.

Rambisai: (Getting nearer and shouting). And you are women! You old woman! How can you say you are Chenjerai when you are a woman? Do you want to disparage us? We are not joking. There are numerous thieves in this area these days, and we were thinking you are thieves. Now jokes aside. Tell us your names, where you come from and where you are going. Traditionally, true visitors don't stay by the cattle pen, like you have done.

Tete: That's fine. It seems you didn't understand my language. This one by my side, in quilt (pointing at Maidei) is Maidei, my brother's daughter. She was impregnated by Chenjerai. That's why you heard me saying: 'I am Chenjerai'. As per our laid down traditions, myself as her aunt has brought her to her new home- where she was damaged. So here is your wife Chenjerai (Pointing at Maidei).

Chenjerai: But Maidei, I told you that I am married! How did you get preg…..? (Rambisai interrupts).

Rambisai: (Panting). Shut up Chenjerai! Stupid! So you mean what this woman (pointing at Tete) said is true? He-e! So all those days you leave home saying you are going for a drink; this is the beer you meant? (Pointing at Maidei). He-e! Tell me!

Chenjerai: A-ah! I just slept with her twice. After all I told her I am married. I do not know why she got pre.... (Rambisai slapping Chenjerai on the right cheek).

Rambisai: Eish, Idiot! You are not even embarrassed! A married man! What don't you get from me which you get from other women? Were you told she has a sweeter 'pot of honey' than me? (pointing at Maidei). Or did someone lie to you that prostitutes are treated with sugar? Tell me! Or is there any single day I refused to….? You are not even ashamed! This is how you men bring us AIDS. You always ask for money to go drinking when in fact you want to go and pay prostitutes? Now you women (pointing at Tete and Maidei), here you have no place at all. You made a very big mistake to play with a married man. His 'joy stick' only belongs to me and me alone! You know the path that led you here. Stand up and go back now!

Tete: You silly woman (pointing at Rambisai), calm down! What are you now talking about? We didn't come here for you. You better keep quite! Did you ever impregnate any woman when you are also a woman? Hold yourself. The owner of the pregnancy is here. (Pointing at Chenjerai). He knows what he did to my child. I wanted to sleep for at least a day, but now I have made up my mind. Chenejrai! This is your wife. If you want to kill her, to beat her, to take her to your bedroom … It's all up to you. Maidei my child, this is your home…and that is your husband. (Pointing at Chenjerai). Come hard time, come joy, you stay here. Off I go! (Standing).

Rambisai: (Panting). You are even giving orders as if you are at your own homestead. Where is she going to stay? This is my home. We constructed together with my husband, not with your child. If you have heard him (pointing at Chenjerai) saying Mai Rudo, I am the one. (Pointing at her chest). I don't tolerate any nonsense at my home. She goes where she was impregnated. If in the bushes, she will go and stay in the bushes. If in the bar, she will go and stay in the bar, not here at my home. You bring her here, did she told you that she was impregnated in any of my houses?

Tete: He-e he-e da! Why do you make me laugh as if all is well with me? Whether you like it not, I will leave her behind. This homestead belongs to Chenjerai. Not you. Chenjerai! Here is your wife. (Pointing at Maidei). Stay well. We will meet again the day you come to pay lobola. I am now leaving. (Turning her back).

Chenjerai: Tete! I beg you to stay for a moment so that we discuss the way forward. Please wait Tete. I want to know how….. (Rambisai point fingers at him, and he keeps quite).

Rambisai: Hey you Chenje! Chenje! Are you crazy? Who has bewitched you? What do you want to discuss with her? Tell me! Do you mean you accept responsibility of the pregnancy? He-e! Hey you, remove your quilt and follow your aunt. (Referring to Maidei). Go! Fatser before I work you out. Chenje is already occupied. You understand? (Pointing at Rambisai with her knobkerrie).

Tete: Chenje! I have played my part. It's now all up to you. If you want to kill her (Pointing at Maidei), but her avenging spirit will wreak havoc in your family. You know the *ngozi* of a pregnant woman! It will sweep you all. I have already bid farewell, I will not say bye again. (Leaving).

Chenjerai: (Calmly). Calm down Rambisai. We are already in problems. We need to negotiate with them. A case can never be settled through a fight.

Rambisai: Chenje! You make me crazy. Are you still in your right mind? Or what did they give you that make you think like a toddler? Now if you think that your prostitute will find a place here, forget. Hey you thigh vendor remove your quilt and go (Forcelfully taking away the quilt from Maidei's head). Follow your aunt before it is too late. Faster! (Kicking Maidei). I told you long back that you have no place here. Even to sleep a single day. If you stay behind you will sleep outside, I tell you. Oh, I swear! And you know there are hyenas these days. These will wake you up if you are a stupid.

Chenje, let's go. Leave that prostitute alone. (Dragging Chenjerai back home).

Maidei: You want me to go back with Tete when I have Chenjerai's pregnancy? What am I going to do with his pregnancy? I will stay here!

Chenjerai: Eh Mai Rudo! Why can't you let her sleep just for today? She will go tomorrow morning. Look! Her aunt has already gone. You know this area is infested with dangerous wild animals. If she sleeps outside here, certainly she will be attacked by hyenas. She will then fight us back as an avenging spirit. I don't want *ngozi* in my family! (Rambisai continues dragging Chenjerai by hand).

Rambisai: If this is what you planned together, you played yourselves. You can't play me such cheap tricks. I told her long back to follow her aunt. If she doesn't want, leave her alone. She will sleep there, and hyenas will wake her up. That's when she will know married men are not the right people to open their 'gates' for. (Maidei stays behind and then follow up her aunt).

Stage II

(Maidei is on her way from Pasai business centre. She meets Takurai along the way. Takurai proposes love from Maidei in spite of her being 3 months pregnant).

Takurai: Hallo Maidei! I have been terribly looking for you. Where have you been all these days?

Maidei: (Frightened and turning her head backwards). Ah, hey Taku! You frighten me. You just appear from nowhere like a ghost! (Smiling).

Takurai: Ah-a, don't you know that a man with real love picks up the scent of a woman he loves?

Maidei: You are lying! Someone told you that I have gone to the grinding mill with a wheelbarrow. You couldn't have foretell or smell my scent as you are saying. You can't be like a dog that picks up the prey's scent. (Stopping her wheelbarrow to settle back her sack that is almost falling).

Takurai: Let me push the wheelbarrow for you. We will talk as we walk. When tired, we will see where we can stop while I tell you the story I have brought you.

Maidei: Don't trouble yourself Taku. I will push my wheelbarrow alone. Besides, I don't want to delay you where you are going. You can go your way. (Giving way to Takurai).

Takurai: Which way are you talking about Maidei? You are my cause of being here. Revai, your aunt's son is the one who told me that you have gone to Pasai business centre. I then took my way here without delay. I was afraid I would not be able to meet you if I delay. When I got at the grinding meal, I heard that you had just left for home. I started running in order to find you before reaching home. Now I am happy that I have met you.

Maidei: Is everything okay that you hunt me like a rabbit? You came to my aunt's homestead. Now you are here looking for me! (Anxiously).

Takurai: It's all well Maidei. Only my heart that is more like a spoon that overturn hot stuff. You know since last year when I proposed love to you, my heart never settled down. You declined my proposal but it never went well with me. When I heard that you went to marry Chenjerai, to be his second wife, I almost bursted with anger. I cried. If it were not my friend, Jealous, you could have seen me following you up. When I later on heard that Chenjerai chased you away, I said to myself: 'God has heard my prayers'. I love you Maidei. This is still my song to you- the reason why you see me here.

Maidei: (Giving a sigh of relief). I hear your words Taku, but it's already too late. It's no longer possible for us to fall in love.

Takurai: (Looking miserably). Come on Maidei! Don't tell me this. You know when I heard you are back from Chenjerai's home, I celebrated with joy. Since last month when I heard you are back, I have been hunting you that we resume our talks. How can you say it's now impossible when Chenjerai divorced you? Do you mean you already had another boyfriend other than me?

Maidei: Um! You know marriage issues are too complex and tricky. I am no longer interested in anything along those lines. *'Makudo ndimamwe'/* Men are the same. You are no good at all. You promise someone everlasting love, marriage and even wedding. But when there is pregnancy you appear as if you were never involved- as if the woman got the pregnancy from heaven. I think I would be happy if you leave me alone. I want to stay like this. I no longer want to hear about love from any man. So if you want to talk with me, we better change the subject. Ok! (Carrying on with her wheelbarrow).

Takurai: Maidei! It's like you are piercing me with a needle right at the heart. The problem is if one baboon destroys a farmer's garden, all other baboons are labelled likewise. But remember it's not all men who do what you said. Our elders usually say: *"Chembere yokwaChivi yakabika mabwe ikamwa muto"* (The Chivi old woman cooked stones and drank the soup). Why can't you try me and see if I will not give you all thee love you deserve? Do you think if I did not love you wholeheartedly, I would have kept on chasing you? Truly, I could have looked for a different woman to marry. But, I couldn't because I love you for sure. (Maidei stops her wheelbarrow, talking).

Maidei: I am hearing your words Taku, but I said it's now impossible for us to fall in love, especially considering my status. It's too late.

Takurai: What status Maidei! For me even if you had successfully married Chenjerai and bear two or three children before you divorce, I still loved you. If I fail to marry you, I think I will better stay a bachelor for ever. I do not think I

51

will ever find someone I love the way I do to you. I love you Maidei. I love you!

Maidei: I do understand you very well, but it seems you don't understand my language. I am saying, even if I were to fall in love with you it's no longer possible. I am already pregnant. I was impregnated by Chenjerai and then he divorced me- sending me away like a dog. That's fine, but God knows. I am three months pregnant now. (Raising 3 fingers up).

Takurai: That is what I have said before Maidei. That's not an issue at all. I told you that even if you were to be divorced after three children, I still loved you. Once you accept my proposal, I will not take long before marrying you. I loved you a long time ago, and my heart burns for you.

Maidei: But even if you love me, could it still be possible that a bachelor like you who never married fall in love and get married to an old woman like me? Though we might be of almost the same age, I am now an old woman considering my current status.

Takurai: Maidei! I have always wanted you to be the Princess of my house. You are my ideal woman. So, I really mean it when I say don't worry about that. What matters is love. I love you with all my heart. Can't you tell me good news?

Maidei: Um! Eh...eh...But even if I tell you that I love you, where am I going to put this pregnancy? (Pointing at her stomach). Would you accept to care for another man's child? That's where my worry is.

Takurai: Once you accept my proposal - that you love me - I will care for you and your child. I have no problem with that. In fact once we marry each other we are now one flesh. What belongs to you also belongs to me, and vice versa. So, I will care for your child the same way I will do to the children we are going to have together. So shall I rejoice?

Maidei: (Smiling and her eyes radiating). With those promises, yes you can rejoice. I love you, but please don't let me down. Otherwise, all my relatives especially my aunt will not stand by my side anymore. I will be an outcast in the family as they would all think I have chosen to become a prostitute.

Takurai: (Hugging Maidei). I am more than happy to hear your comforting words Maidei- words I have always been longing to hear from you for too long now. It's only today that my heart has settled. Never ever think that I will let you down, yourself and the child you are carrying. I will care for you, and give you all the love you deserve. Very soon I will marry you before you change your mind. (Smiling). Let me help you push the wheelbarrow to your aunt's home. I need to go back where I am working. I didn't tell anyone that I am coming after you. I just left without informing anyone. They will soon start looking for me. (Pushing Maidei's wheelbarrow).

Stage III

(People are gathered at Takurai's homestead in chief Chitsa. It is after the death of Takurai who untimely died in a car accident. They are sharing the deceased, Takurai's estate according to the Shona tradition. Mubvandiripo, the "eldest son" of the deceased is denied the right to inherit "his father's" estate for a reason he is only hearing for the first time, that he is a step-child).

Babamukuru: (Welcoming the deceased's relatives as per the Shona custom). I am so sorry for the untimely death of my younger brother, Takurai. (Some tears). Anyway, it's beyond our control, and every one of us will go the same way. We will all ultimately follow our ancestors. Well, we all know that our relative sleeping there (pointing at Takurai's grave) left an estate and a family that still need to go on with life. As such, I shall ask our eldest nephew, Govai to divide the estate between family members as per our tradition kinship. But since the deceased left children who still need support, I am going to ask Govai to share clothes only. All other assets/properties will be set aside for the children and wife of the deceased. Over to you Govai! (Turning his head to Govai).

Govai: (Welcoming people according to tradition). Thank you uncle! Without wasting much of your time, let me quickly do my work. (Spraying the deceased's property with traditional medicine). This knobkerrie, we will hand over to Tichatonga, the eldest son of the deceased. It's a sign that he will be responsible for the administration of his father's home and estate – "sarapavana". (Mubvandiripo is surprised. He shakes his head in disapproval before he stands up to speak).

Mubvandiripo: (Flabbergasted). Hey you Govai! Are you drunk or crazy? You can't forget that I am Takurai's eldest son! How many children are there between me and Tichatonga? Two sisters! And, you forget so easily that I am the one who should take over the administration of my father's estate? Think well before….. (Govai interrupts fumingly).

Govai: Hey Mubvandiripo! Get out of my business! I am neither drunk nor crazy as you think. I do what I know. I don't want to believe that you know my work more than I do. How can you ask me obvious things? You ask me what you certainly know? Do you want to change your identity only now? (Mubvandiripo, fierce like the arrow of a scorpion jumps closer to Govai).

Mubvandiripo: Govai! Govai! Stupid moron! You must be up to something damning! What identity are you talking about? You think I am a woman or what? He-e! Did I tell you that I do not want to be responsible for my father's estate? Answer me, you idiot! (Seizing Govai by the neck. Babamukuru intervenes).

Babamukuru: (Getting hold of Mubvandiripo's right hand). My son, you can't settle a case through fighting. Violence begets violence. Look! We are still mourning, and you want to start over another problem. If there is something you didn't understand, all you have to do is to ask your elders. We will clarify everything to you. You understand son? Don't be violent. (Govai interrupts).

Govai: Uncle! A child who cries for fire should be left to burn. Let him do what he wants to do. Don't hold him back.

This is not my first time to administer an estate! I will let him take all he wants if he is longing to die like a donkey. This is the deceased's estate? He wants to grow from grass to grace that easy? Well, I am giving you a blank check- I am no longer in charge. (Moving away from the deceased's property). Let him do as he pleases! If he wants a fight, I am here! I will give him what he deserves. If he wants my uncle's estate, let him take. He will die like a dog. (Referring to Mubvandiripo).

Babamukuru: Not that Govai! (Letting go Mubvandiripo, and holding back Govai). You will spoil everything. What you need to do is to explain him, not quarrelling and fighting. You are now an adult person with wealth of experiences. Explain to him peacefully, not invoking his anger.

Govai: What should I explain to him uncle? Didn't you tell him everything before? Even grandma, his mother, I am sure she told him! Should I keep on telling him what he already know? That would make no sense.

Mubvandiripo: Telling me what? You people, is this a pre-planned thing? Even babamukuru, you seem to be on the side of Govai! What are you saying he should tell me? And I seem to be the only one in the darkness!

Babamukuru: No my son! Calm down. We will sit down and talk. Govai! (Pointing at Govai). Please stop what you are doing, we need to talk before things slip out of hand. Mubvandiripo, yourself, Mbuya, Maidei, aunt Rhoda and myself, come let's talk. All other relatives, I am sure you all see what is happening here. I am sorry for taking your precious time, but we need to settle the dust first. Please don't go away. Just hang around here. We will resume the exercise very soon- as soon as the dust is settled. (Noise as people temporarily disperse).

Mbuya: I didn't know your case will be all this trouble! Maidei, didn't you inform your child? (Mubvandiripo perplexed, and then asks).

Mubvandiripo: There seem to be something all of you know except me! What is it?

Babamukuru: (Pointing at Maidei). Eh *mainini*, did you ever told Mubvandiripo the truth about things here at home? Or my deceased brother, Takura, did he tell him before passing on?

Maidei: (Shaking her head). No, I didn't. Neither did Takurai do. (Everyone except Mubvandiripo and Maidei look astonished. They remain open-mouthed).

Babamukuru: That's why Mubvandiripo demonstrated ignorance, and was unhappy with all the proceedings! It's not his fault. He doesn't know anything. So, please explain to him the real truth now. We are all listening.

Maidei: (Weeping). Can't you tell him babamukuru? I am afraid and ashamed.

Babamukuru: (Clearing his throat). Well, you must be man enough. The news are not for the fainthearted. (Pointing at Mubvandiripo). As confirmed by your mother that you know nothing about what transpired in the past, I will tell you the truth which your mother should have told you a long time ago. The truth is: You are not Takurai's legitimate son. (Mubvandiripo trembling but like a man he gathers courage to listen). Your mother, Maidei was married to Takurai when you were a pregnancy of about four months. That's why you were named 'Mubvandiripo' which means a step-child. My brother, Takurai as someone who was sympathetic, he raised and treated you like his own legitimate son. I am sure this cannot be disputed as your ignorance of this whole truth is in itself a clear testimony that you were treated like any other child here at home. But, we all thought your mother revealed this to you a long time ago as it is always important for a child to know his biological father. A father is like something in one's blood that cannot be condoned without dire consequences.

Mubvandiripo: (Whimpering and then a gaze at his mother as he contemplates the shock of his life). Mum! Mum! Is all this true? (Maidei nods her head in approval, weeping).

Babamukuru: Mubvandiripo, I am sure everything is now clear to you. That's why Govai had done what he did. If anything you still want to know, feel free to ask. We want to go ahead with what we are gathered for ….Eh people are waiting for us.

Mubvandiripo: (His palm on his right cheek). So mum, why didn't you tell me the truth all these years? I am now 19 with such truth concealed in your heart? You are a real witch! Today you will know my real colour. (Standing up with clinched fists to punch Maidei, but is held back by Babamukuru).

Babamukuru: My son. You are making a terrible mistake. I told you before that violence beget violence and, adoration begets adoration. Just a word of advice: Two wrongs cannot make a right. The best thing to do now is to peacefully ask your mother about the whereabouts of your real father. You understand! If you beat her, how is she going to tell you all this? You are grown up son. Play your cards carefully.

Mubvandiripo: (Now a bit calm). Mother! So who is my real father, and where he lives?

Maidei: (Weeping and stammering). He- he- is- Che- Che- Chenjerai Nha- Nhamo. He divorced me when I was 3 months your pregnant.

Mubvandiripo: (With a loud voice). I asked, 'Where does he live?'

Maidei: In- in- in chief Zi- Ziki's area.

Mubvandiripo: So all this time, you made me look after an estate which you knew I have no share? You made me a servant of your husband's house! But why mum? Why? Is this what you wanted? That I am ashamed, and made a laughing stock before this entire crowd? You knew very well that Takurai was not my real father, but never dared letting me know! Even a single day! What did you want my life to become? Why didn't you take me to my father's house all this long? At least to show me his face! Is this what you were waiting for? A lifetime humiliation? (Threshing himself on the ground whimpering, and then rises up to track down the foot prints of his real father).

Scene 2

(Mubvandiripo arrives at his [real] father, Chenjerai Nhamo's home in chief Ziki's area. It is after Chenjerai's burial and people are seated under the shade of a Muchakata tree to deliberate on the deceased's estate).

Mubvandiripo: (Arriving at Chenjerai's homestead). Go-go-goi! *Tisvikewo*!

Babamunini: Yes, come on! But, we are a family somehow busy here. Or let me take you aside and hear what you have brought us. Excuse me just a moment (referring to the crowd), I want to talk to that gentleman. Come along gentleman (Pointing at Mubvandiripo). Let us sit here. (Pointing at a log just a few metres from the crowd).

Mubvandiripo: I am sorry father for interrupting. (Staring at Babamunini).

Babamunini: It's not a very big problem son. Only that we are not familiar to each other. Who are you, and what have brought you here?

Mubvandiripo: Well, my name is Mubvandiripo. I come from Chitsa, in Gutu, and am looking for my father named Chenjerai Nhamo. I have heard that this is his home, but I am surprised to see a crowd of people. Is there a party?

Babamunini: (Startled). Are you sure you are Chenjerai's son?

61

Mubvandiripo: Yes, I am!

Babamunini: It's very strange! Do you know Chenjerai if you see him?

Mubvandiripo: I am not familiar with his face, but that is his name.

Babamunini: Hey son! So how can you look for a father you are not familiar with? Besides, you must be in your early twenties or late teens. What were you doing all along to look for your father only now?

Mubvandiripo: What has made me wondering like this is the passion to know my father.

Babamunini: That is what I have asked you son. Has that passion had an effect on you only now when you are as old as you are?

Mubvandiripo: (Sobbing). No, my father. The story is very long, and a sad one to remember.

Babamunini: What the cry is all about my son? Is this what you called me for? Behave like a man. A real man doesn't cry. Be steady and narrate your story.

Mubvandiripo: (A bit composed). I was informed only 3 days ago by my mother that the father I grew up with is not my real father. My real father is Chenjerai Nhamo. (Whimpering. Maonei, Chenjerai's mother have a sense that all is not well between the new comer and his son. She goes there).

Maonei: Eh my son (referring to Babamunini), people are waiting! And, it seems this other one here is crying! Who is he and what have you done to him?

Babamunini: It's good that you have come mum. The story here is complex. I won't be able to digest it alone. Would you kindly call up aunt Marujata. You also need to be here with us. (Referring to his mother).

Maonei: What kind of story that requires even the aunt to be here? (Looking at Mubvandiripo's face). Ah-a! And, who is this boy who resembles my son, Chenjerai? This is a bizarre! (Sitting down to understand more, and with an eye on Mubvandiripo).

Babamunini: Mum! Just call them so that we talk over it together.

Maonei: (Standing). Well, let me call them that we hear the story!

VaMarujata: (Seating down). Is everything well here? I heard my in-law calling me.

Babamunini: Ehe-e aunt, I am the one who have called you up. There is an issue I want us to discuss together. It's about our son here. (Pointing at Mubvandiripo).

Marujata: Ah, and it was before greeting you my son! (Referring to Mubvandiripo). (Extending her hand to Mubvandiripo).

Mubvandiripo: (Extending his hand). Hallo grandma. How are you doing?

Marujata: (Her hand on her open mouth). Ah-a! Is this a mirage or reality? Do you see what I am seeing? (Referring to Maonei). Is this Chenjerai who has risen? They are very much alike!

Babamunini: Aunt, your attention please! We don't have time. Look, all those people are waiting for us.

Marujata: Yes Chirandu, we are listening. (Looking at Babamunini). Go ahead.

Babamunini: Aunt, mum, and Rambisai, the reason why I have summoned you here is this boy. (Pointing at Mubvandiripo).

Marujata: What has he done? (Hands on her stomach).

Babamunini: This boy (pointing at Mubvandiripo) is looking for his father. Now when I asked him the name of his father, he said it's Chenjerai Nhamo. I asked him the reason why he thought of looking for his father only now, and he said he only came to know a few days ago that the father who raised him was not his real father. He was told by his mother that his real father is Chenjerai Nhamo.

Marujata: (She stands up and starts dancing). This is what I told you before! That Chenjerai has risen. No difference between him and Chenje! An ancestors' call! The child who was lost all these years have been called home by his own father. (Ululating).

Babamunini: Don't rush aunt! Rushing does not ensure safe arrival. Sit down, and let us discuss the matter. Did you pass through Mr Tande where they put *cannabis sativa* in beer? Let us hear from the horse's mouth. You can tell us your story son. We are all listening. (Looking at Mubvandiripo).

Mubvandiripo: (Standing). My name is Mubvandiripo. I am looking for my father named Chenjerai Nhamo, and I am told this is his homestead.

Babamunini: I had already asked you the reason why you thought of going after your father only now. But I didn't tell you that as far as we know the Chenjerai you are talking about has never had two wives. Perhaps you are referring to a different Chenjerai. What is the name of your mother?

Mubvandiripo: The name of my mother is Maidei Munyama. According to her, she was impregnated by my father Chenjerai Nhamo who was already a family man. When she was 3 months pregnant, she eloped, but was chased away by my father's elder wife. She said, my father's elder wife was Rumbi or Rambisai….something like that. The reason why I delay coming is that my mother only told me of all this last week after her husband passed on. (Stunned, the trio looks at each other silently). That is when it was revealed that I was a step-son to the deceased.

Marujata: (Kneeling and talking to ancestors). Yes my ancestors! You said your offspring cannot perish in the forest. You have done a wonderfully good thing! But why this late! Look he comes only to see the other has just departed!

Babamunini: Aunt, let us solve the issue first! We are not yet 100 per cent sure if this is Chenjerai's son. And, mum you have heard his side of the story. What do you think?

Maonei: They hear my son, they don't till. (Touching her ears). Do you think anyone who knows Chenjerai can dispute that this is his son? (Pointing at Mubvandiripo). But even though, we still need to hear from Rambisai for confirmation. Perhaps she knows something about this child. If she prophecy ignorance on the matter, then, we would need to take other measures. Otherwise, we accept someone who is not part of us.

Babamunini: (Smiling). That's why our elders used to say: "One finger cannot crush a louse". You have given us an excellent contribution. Let me just call Rambisai right away. (Calling).

Rambisai: (Kneeling before Babamunini). Here I am Babamunini.

Babamunini: It's me who has called you up. There is an issue we are discussing here. It's about this boy. (Pointing at Mubvandiripo). He said he is the son of Chenjerai. Her mother is Maidei. Do you know him or did you ever hear about him?

Rambisai: (Looking at Mubvandiripo, and scratching her head). Um….his face is not familiar to me, but I know the story of Maidei. She came to marry my husband when she was 2 or 3 months pregnant, but I couldn't allow her to stay. She left that time but never came back. As to whether she later on gave birth to a baby boy or a baby girl, that much I don't know. That's all what I know.

Babamunini: That's fine *amaiguru*. It's all we wanted to know. You can go back.

Rambisai: (Standing). That's fine, thank you.

Babamunini: I am sure we have all heard Rambisai's confirmation. Initially I had thought of sending back Mubvandiripo to bring his mother, but given that his words have been confirmed by Rambisai I think there is no longer any need to do that. Besides, he has many similar features with Chenjerai that one can hardly dispute he is son to Chenjerai. Isn't it aunt and mum?

Maonei and Marujata: (One voice). That's it! He is Chenjerai himself!

Babamunini: So I think we can formally tell him the cause of our gathering here because he knows nothing yet. Aunt you can tell him.

Marujata: (Sobbing). I am sorry to tell you that your father, Chenjerai has just joined his ancestors. He passed on last week after a short illness. We only led him to rest a day before yesterday. And, now we are gathering to deliberate on his estate. I am very sorry son....hi-i hi-i hi-i. (Crying).

Mubvandiripo: (Threshing himself on the ground, whimpering). Maiwe! Mama! Do I have a misfortune of an owl that if it travels in the night they say: "It's a witch". If it travels during the day it is struck by other birds. My father! Father! Dying before I see your face? Maiwe! Mama!

Babamunini: (Consoling Mubvandiripo). It's over son. That's how life goes. Even if you cry, it no longer helps anymore. You will need to be brave like a man. Ma Rambisai! (Calling Rambisai). Please give your son here some food. He needs to eat and rest for a while. I have to immediately postpone the ceremony for tomorrow after informing all relatives about Mubvandiripo. (Going to meet the crowd).

Stage II

(It is at Chenjerai's homestead again. People have gathered to deliberate on Chenjerai's estate. Mubvandiripo is denied the right to inherit Chenjerai's estate. The kinship/relatives argue he is a son of the forest- *"mwana wemusango"*).

Babamunini: (Speaking to the crowd). My apologies for summoning you twice for an event we could have deliberated on just once. It is because of this child (pointing at Mubvandiripo), one of the late, Chenjerai's sons. As we all know, we only came to know of him on the day we wanted to deliberate on the late person's estate. After explaining his case that was confirmed by Rambisai, the deceased's wife, it came to light that he is Chenjerai's eldest son. Being Chenjerai's eldest son as such, we saw it fit not to deliberate on the former's estate before settling down his case. For those relatives who didn't know the reason why the last session was adjourned, this was the reason. Now, I am going to ask our eldest nephew, Enzanisai to preside over this ceremony. Over to you Enzanisai! (Turning onto Enzanisai).

Enzanisai: (Standing and greeting the crowd). Thank you uncle! We all know this is an adjudicator's task, and it's no easy task. But, I hope I will be able to satisfy everyone. (Spraying the deceased's property with liquid medicine). This knobkerrie, I will give to Takudzwa, the deceased's eldest son.

Mubvandiripo: (Flummoxed). I just stood up to remind you that I am Chenjerai's eldest son as has just been announced by Babamunini. I should believe it was just a slip of the tongue when you said Takudzwa. So..... (He is interrupted by Enzanisai).

Enzanisai: Let me do my work as I know. I haven't forgotten anything at all. The truth is I can't give a knobkerrie to a forest child because.... (Mubvandiripo grabs him by the neck).

Mubvandiripo: (Trembling with anger). Me! The real and legitimate eldest son of Chenjerai! And, you call me a forest child-mwana wemusango? Do you know a forest child? (Babamunini intervenes).

Babamunini: Ah-a! What the noise, quarrels and *jambanja* all for? This is a ritual ceremony that should be conducted peacefully. Ancestors won't like this. Had we knew that this is what you (pointing at Mubvandiripo) were going to do; we couldn't have accepted you as a member of this family. We were simply going to say: "We know you not". So sit down, and let the nephew do his job. If you have a query, you will raise it later not now.

Enzanisai: (With eyes wide open). Hey uncle Pedzisai! Leave him alone! Don't hold him back. He think I can be all that blind to give fatherly responsibility to a forest child leaving behind those who worked and cared for the deceased's estate? Hey you Mubvandiripo! You must be an idiot who think money grow on trees. You must teach your itch for luxury how to behave. If you do not know, a forest child benefits from the family where he is raised. That's where you wasted your energies, not here. Here, you have no share. You want to reap where you did not scatter even a single seeds? You...... (Babamunini intervenes).

Babamunini: You don't have to talk like that Enzanisai! A nephew is an adjudicator, and that's not how adjudicators behave. Besides, you are now bald-headed, a sign that you are a holder of vast experiences and wisdom. Where are the experiences and wisdom then? All you should do is to explain clearly to him. He is still a child, and he has the right to know why this and that have been done. Go ahead with your work. My son (pointing at Mubvandiripo), you can sit down.

Mubvandiripo: (Crying loudly). Hi-i hi-i hi-i, Maiwe! Mama! So what will I inherit on this earth? Am I a curse to everyone? Where I grew up they denied me the right to become heir to the estate I toiled for. They said I can't inherit anything because I am a step-child. Now I come home, my legitimate home, where I should get a lion's share. I am labelled a forest child. So what shall become of me on this poor earth? Besides, sweat and tears, what else shall I inherit on this earth? Like a disease, I am rejected by everyone. It's like I am following a shadow that flies! Hi-i hi-i hi-i! Maiwe! (Mubvandiripo threshes himself on the ground whimpering. The ceremony is suspended as people attend to him).

-END-